KEEPERS OF THE
BODY

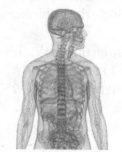

A Call to Unity

DIANE WHITE

ISBN 978-1-63885-777-8 (Paperback)
ISBN 978-1-63885-778-5 (Digital)

Covenant Books, Inc.
11661 Hwy 707
Murrells Inlet, SC 29576
www.covenantbooks.com

CONTENTS

INTRODUCTION

The body of Christ has operated over the years as if we are an island all to ourselves. Many congregations are only concerned about those in their ministry that regularly attend their services while less concern is given to those who are members that attend periodically. Little to no concern is given to the many lost souls that live within the vicinity of their church that is passed each time they enter into their church buildings. There is also extraordinarily little concern given to other churches in the same area, especially if they are a part of a different organized group. Unfortunately, there is no urgency for churches in the same area to come together to win their area for Christ. In fact, the truth be told, there is sometimes competition between churches as they fight to entice each other's members to switch to their church while overlooking those outside the church that is waiting to be invited in.

In the fourth chapter of Genesis, the spirit of jealousy that now exists in the churches was birthed between two brothers. After the fall of mankind, Adam and Eve had two sons, Cain and Abel. After they had become men, both men presented their offering of worship unto God, and Cain observed his brother, Abel's worship, and God's response to Abel's worship. Cain saw the relationship that Abel had with God and became jealous first and then angry. Because God is no respecter of person, and does not value one person more than another, Cain had the same availability to reach God as Abel did.

But instead, Cain grew to hate his brother for no other reason than his worship was authentic and pure. God required a blood sacrifice, and while Abel, a keeper of sheep, provided a blood sacrifice, Cain, a tiller of the ground, gave God a sacrifice of the fruit of the ground. Abel did not slack on his worship and gave God what was required, and God received it. Cain, on the other hand, did not give God the worship that was required, so his offering was not received. Cain hated his brother's relationship with God so much that he killed Abel. Genesis 4:9 says that the Lord said to Cain, "Where is Abel your brother?" Cain's response was, "I do not know. Am I my brother's keeper?" God knew what Cain had done to Abel before He asked him about his brother. God knew because as He told Cain, "The voice of your brother's blood cries out to Me from the ground."

Today, we go on in life doing ministry and having church as we deem necessary. But have we considered that there may be voices calling out to God because of our neglect of their needs and that this neglect may be killing them? This book is written to the body of Christ to look at the questions, "Am I my brother's keeper?" Are we responsible for our brother's well-being? Can I excel in ministry as I watch my brother spiral down to disaster? It is searching of the Holy Scriptures to see what God says to us regarding these questions. This is not a gender-specific question but is relevant to every person in the body of Christ.

God is calling us to unity—to be one body. God provides instruction on the means through which we can be united. However, these instructions are overshadowed by the belief that we can function properly on our own. Most of us passionately believe that all we need is God on our side to accomplish our assigned tasks. We take no notice that we really need others in our lives as well. We move forward trying to operate in a bubble isolated from all others. God intended that we would operate as one functioning body; each part needing the other part to function effectively.

Hezekiah Walker wrote a song that many congregations sing during worship. But are we taking the words of the song to heart because they are really true?

> I need you, you need me,
> We're all a part of God's Body.
> Stand with me, agree with me.
> We're all a part of God's Body.
> It is His will that every need be provided.
> You are important to me; I need you to survive.

CHAPTER 1

How Our Natural Body Functions

What comes first is the natural body, then
the spiritual body come later.
—1 Corinthians 15:46 (NLT)

Though this is a book about the body of Christ, keeping in mind the words of 1 Corinthians 15:46, there are some insights that we can gain as we look at the natural body. Understanding the natural body that God created is important. It shows how God also intended the body of Christ to operate. God purposely calls us the body of Christ because of His intentions for us. The natural body is many parts working together to make the body function efficiently. Could that be why God calls us the body of Christ? Are we supposed to work together to function efficiently?

In our natural body, our bones give our body support and structure. They protect our internal organs.

The brain controls the body's functions. The biggest part of the brain is the cerebrum, which takes up 85 percent of the brain. Below the cerebrum at the back of the brain is the cerebellum. It controls balance, movement, and coordination of our muscles. In the front of the cerebellum is the brain stem. It connects the brain to the spinal cord. It is in charge of the activities that keep the body alive, such as breathing air, digesting food, circulating the blood, and controlling the involuntary muscles in the heart and stomach.

The pituitary gland in the brain is the size of a pea, and it controls growth. Its job is to produce and release hormones into the body. It also controls the amount of sugar and water in the body and helps keep the metabolism going.

The hypothalamus in the brain controls the body's temperature. If the body is too hot, it tells the body to sweat. If the body is too cold, it gives the body shivers.

The digestive system consists of the parts of the body that work together to turn food and liquids into the building blocks and fuel that the body needs. The parts involved in this digestive system are the mouth, tongue, esophagus, muscles in the esophagus, stomach, small intestine, pancreas, liver, gallbladder, large intestine, and appendix. All these parts work separately to do their part but collectively as the digestive system.

The endocrine system tells the cells in your body what to do. The glands in this system are the endocrine glands, the pituitary gland (known as the master gland), the thyroid gland, the adrenal gland (that creates adrenaline), and the pancreas (the largest endocrine gland). Like the digestive system, each gland has a separate function that works collectively to make the endocrine system function effectively.

The ears are in charge of collecting sounds, processing the sounds, and sending sound signals to the brain. They also help you to keep your balance whenever you bend over.

The eyes allow you to see. They take in information about the world around and then sends this information to the brain. Also involved in the process of getting information from the eyes to the brain are the eyelids and parts of the eye: the sclera, cornea, iris, retina, and rods and cones. The rods and cones are the cells in the retina that process light. The rods process black and white, and the cones process color. The lacrimal gland in the eye makes tears.

Hair is not only on your head but also all over the body. Some hair is easy to see; others are almost invisible. Depending on where the hair is located determines its job. For example, hair on the head keeps the head warm, hair in the nose protect the nose and the lungs, whereas eyelashes protect the eyes.

The heart and the circulatory system consist of many parts. The heart is a muscle. It sends blood around the body. The blood provides the body with the oxygen and nutrients it needs plus it carries away waste. The heart is made of four different chambers. The two chambers on top are called the atria. They receive the blood returning to the heart from the body and lungs. The two chambers on the bottom called the ventricles squirt out the blood to the body and the lungs. Down the middle of the heart is the septum.

Although separated by the septum, the atria and ventricles work as a team. The heart has valves that help the flow of the blood. The mitral valve, tricuspid valve, aortic valve, and pulmonary valve all work together to keep the blood flowing forward. The blood flows through the blood vessels attached to the heart. The vessels that carry blood away from the heart are the arteries. The ones that carry blood back to the heart are the veins.

The system in the body that helps fight off sickness is the immune system. The immune system is made up of a network of cells, tissues, and organs that work together to protect the body. White blood cells are part of the defense system. There are two types of these cells. One type chews up invading germs. The other type allows the body to remember and recognize previous invaders. Clusters of immune system cells are in the lymph nodes. The lymph nodes work like filters to remove germs that could make the body sick.

The lungs are one of the largest organs, and they work with the respiratory system to take in the fresh air, get rid of stale air, and talk. The lung on the left side is smaller than the lung on the right side to allow room for the heart. The lungs are protected by the rib cage. Beneath the lungs is the diaphragm, a muscle that works with the lungs to allow for inhaling and exhaling air. Inside the lungs are the windpipes, bronchi, the tiniest tubes called bronchioles, tiny air sacs called alveoli, and small blood vessels called capillaries.

The body has over six hundred muscles. These muscles do everything from pumping blood throughout the body to helping the body lift heavy objects. Some muscles are controlled while others do their job automatically. Smooth muscles are told what to do by the brain and the body. The heart is a cardiac muscle that functions automatically. Skeletal muscles are voluntary muscles. They are the muscles that can be controlled. Facial muscles are not all attached directly to the bone. Some are attached under the skin, which allows them to be contracted to make different kinds of faces. Major muscles are in the shoulder, upper chest, abdomen, arms, biceps, front of the thigh, and the bottom.

The nose allows for smelling and is a big part of being able to taste. The nose is the main gate to the respiratory system. The nose has two holes called the nostrils. Behind the nose is the nasal cavity. It connects with the back of the throat. The nasal cavity is separated from the inside of your mouth by the palate. The nose is how air leaves the body when you exhale. Inside the nose is the mucous membrane that warms up the air and moistens it. The mucous membrane creates mucus that captures dust, germs, and other small particles that could irritate the lungs.

On the roof of the nasal cavity is the olfactory epithelium. It contains special receptors that are sensitive to odor, molecules that travel through the air. The brain interprets the combination of receptors to recognize different smells. Without the nose, you can't taste anything. The ability to smell and taste go together because odors allow for a fuller taste.

The skin holds everything together. It protects the body and keeps the body at just the right temperature. It also allows the body to have the sense of touch.

The tongue is used to chew, swallow, talk, and taste. The tongue is made up of many groups of muscles. These muscles run in different directions to carry out all the jobs of the tongue. The tongue has ten thousand taste buds that can detect sweet, sour, bitter, and salty. The back of the tongue contains the lingual tonsil, which helps filter out harmful germs that could cause an infection in the body.

This is a substantial amount of information about the body, yet it is not all-inclusive. Many parts of the body were not included, or there was a limited amount of information provided for those parts that were covered. The point to take away from all this information is that God created our bodies with so many intricate parts that work together or affect the workings of other parts of the body. Some parts work to perform their separate tasks as well as work together as a system. Other parts work separately but another part relies on their operability to complete their assigned task. Our natural bodies and its workings are reflective of the body of Christ. In the body of Christ, there are also many parts that work together for it to function properly. Just like our natural body, the body of Christ is many parts that make up one body, and the body of Christ needs all parts working efficiently for the whole body to function efficiently.

References

www.healthline.com
www.livescience.com

CHAPTER 2

Coming to Terms with Who We Are

The question of looking at who we are is usually answered by the group that we identify with and with whom we are connected. For instance, we may see ourselves as a Christian, a Baptist, a Catholic, a Methodist, or a Pentecostal. We may further define ourselves as a leader in the church, a supporter, or a member of a specific congregation. All these are a name for a specific group that we identify with but in reality, God has placed us into a group that far outweighs all these groups. The group that God has placed us in is the body of Christ. This group doesn't take into consideration denomination. It doesn't consider whether you are a male or female or whether you are a leader or a lay member, nor does this group take into consideration your ethnicity. God has put us into a group that signifies His feeling toward us and defines how He visualizes each one of us that goes beyond what the natural eye can see.

> I pray that your hearts will be flooded with light so that you can understand the confident hope He has given to those He called—his holy people who are His rich and glorious inheritance. I also pray that you will understand the incredible greatness of God's power for us who believe Him. This is the same mighty power that raise Christ from the dead and seated him in the place

> of honor at God's right hand in the heavenly realms. Now he is far above any ruler or authority, or power of leader or anything else—not only in this world but also in the world to come. God has put all things under the authority of Christ and made him head over all things for the benefit of the Church. And the church is his body, it is made full and complete by Christ, who fills all things everywhere with himself. (Ephesians 1:18–23 NLT)

God, the Father, had a plan, whereby through Jesus Christ and His death on the cross, God restored power to us that was originally lost when mankind first fell into sin in the garden of Eden. He raised Christ from the dead and seated Him at His right hand and put Christ far above all principalities, powers, might, and dominions. And because of Jesus Christ's willingness to submit to the cross, God put all things under His feet and named Him to be the head over all things to the church. The church is what God established as the body of Christ. Jesus is the head of this body, and every Christian, in every place of the world, in every possible denomination, and of all the various races make up the body attached to the head, Jesus Christ.

Before the foundation of the earth, God placed into each person a skill, a calling, a destiny, and his anointing that He deemed necessary for the body of Christ to function properly. The decision of where we function in the body is a God-determined place. Only He really knows what He prepared you to do and where on the body you are needed.

> The human body has many parts, but the many parts make up the whole body, so it is with the body of Christ. Some of us are Jews, some are Gentiles, some are slaves, and some are free. But we have all been baptized into one body by one Spirit, and we all have the same Spirit. Yes, the body has many different parts, not just one part.

If the foot says, "I am not a part of the body because I am not a hand", that does not make it any less a part of the body. And if the ear says," I am not part of the body because I am not an eye", how would you hear? Or if your whole body were an ear, how would you smell anything? But our bodies have many parts, and God has put each part just where he wants it. How strange a body would be if it had only one part! Yes, there are many parts but only one body. The eye can never say to the hand, "I don't need you". The head can't say to the feet, "I don't need you". In fact, some parts of the body that seem weakest and least important are actually the most necessary. And the part we regard as less honorable are those we clothe with the greatest care. So, we carefully protect those parts that should not be seen while the more honorable parts do not require this special care. So, God has put the body together such that extra honor and care are given to those parts that have less dignity. This makes for harmony among the members, so that all the members care for each other. If one part suffers, all parts suffer with it, and if one part is honored, all the parts are glad. All of you together are Christ's body and each of you is a part of it. (1 Corinthians 12:12–27 NLT)

This scripture speaks to how God set up the body of Christ. It confirms that He set up the spiritual body of Christ in just the same manner that He set up the natural body. We are many members with different responsibilities and assignments, but we, together, make up one body. Each part has a function, and it should not look at another part of the body and desire to leave its designated function to take on what that part of the body may consider to be a more desirable function. Mainly because the designated place of each part was designated by God Himself. No part can decide that it will not be a part of the body just because it cannot be the part that it desires to be.

God has set the members as He pleases. He puts into each member what it needs to function as He desires. Similar to those parts of the natural body that automatically perform as they were designed to perform. Perhaps this is what makes certain parts more desirable as one watches them function as they were designed to function. I suppose being visible can be more desirable for a part that works behind the scenes, but can you imagine if the unseen members of your natural body decided it would not function as designed because it would rather be a part of the body that was more visible? Image for a moment if your liver decided it wanted to be the eye, or your heart decided it wanted to be the mouth. Your body would shut down and could not continue to function. So it is with the body of Christ when a member stops doing what God designed them to do.

God never intended for all of us to do the same thing. Even if a member is called to the same position, God made it so that there are different tasks, assignments, and functionalities that require us to work together, though placed in the same position. All members of the body of Christ are needed to make the body function properly. Every member is essential, and it is essential that each member functions at its ultimate level if the body is going to function at its ultimate level. Even the members of the body that are not seen but work in the background are necessary. If they cease to function, the body will not operate efficiently. We have to honor the members of the body without whom the visible parts could not function.

In the natural body, we need our brain, we need our heart, we need our kidneys and liver. All these parts function, but as they work, they are invisible. Similar parts in the body of Christ who give instruction to the other parts of the body behind the scenes, who circulate what is needed to keep the body functioning, and who filter out the unnecessary ideology, customs, and practices in the body are all needed. They may not be recognized because they work behind the scenes, but if these parts don't work, as in the natural, the body will be sick and may even die.

We should pay close attention when a part of our body is defective. The part that is lacking puts more stress on the other parts of the body which affects their ability to operate. Doctors have stressed that early detection and treatment when dealing with the natural body is the best way to be sure that the whole body stays healthy. Spiritually, as the scripture says, if one part of the body suffers, we all suffer, and if one part is honored, we are all honored. When the body of Christ realizes this principle, we will no longer be able to walk past a dysfunctional brother or sister or talk about the struggles of a brother or sister or even watch a brother or sister destroy their destiny without coming to their rescue or at least praying and interceding for them.

Embracing this principle will also kill jealousy within the body because if you win, I win. If you accomplish a great victory, then I, too, am victorious. We are in this together. This is true in the operation of the natural body, and the scripture tells us that it is also true for the body of Christ.

When I personally have a problem with my right knee, I automatically put more stress on my left side. In addition, I also put more stress on both arms and shoulders as I depend on them more to sit down and to stand up because I need them to brace my body because my right knee is not functioning. I've also found that if my knee is down too long, my back begins to hurt because I'm not walking properly either. The same is so when a brother or sister ceases to function the way God designed them to function. Their lack of performance puts more strain on those who have to perform the tasks they were designed to do plus make up the difference for the tasks left undone because of their brother or sister who now can give no input.

The reason for the dysfunction is not really the focus of this book. It is true and has been established that if part of the body is not functioning properly, that lack of efficiency will have a direct effect on every other part of the body of Christ. Therefore, this book focuses on questioning how can any part of the body continue operating without reaching out to a dysfunctional member? Furthermore, how can we think that we are going on to do our ultimate delivery of service to God when our brother and sister are struggling? We must see that God purposely made us connected in such a way that we cannot function properly unless we all function properly. He made us connected in this way so that we would honor and care for each other. So that we would not walk away from a struggling part of the body and leave them to die. He made us keepers of the body.

CHAPTER 3

Understanding Our Parts as a Small Piece of an Enormous Picture

When I think of the kingdom of God and God's plans for His people, I see an enormous tapestry. One like the tapestries in pictures and movies that hung on the walls of old castles, that were hung from the top of the ceiling down to the floor and covered the massive wall. I also see each of us as one little piece of the whole tapestry that embodies not only the body of Christ now but also the body of Christ of the past centuries and those of the future. No matter how God uses us, in reality, we are still just a small piece of the big picture. As we realize how small a piece our assignment represents, it should humble us and change the perspective of how other member's assignments are viewed. We build together, we succeed together, or we fail together.

So often we walk away from a part of the body because of a conflict, disagreement, or hurt. However, we can't cut them off any more than we can cut off our baby toe without experiencing some kind of pain and inability to function properly. I know of someone who lost their baby toe and had to go through rehabilitation to learn how to balance themselves and how to walk without that baby toe. You see, it is small, it is just a baby toe, but it affects the ability to stand and walk. It affects the ability to move. Every part of the body is needed.

We must understand that we do not and cannot stand alone. If my brother or sister is emotionally, mentally, or physically sick, I am sick. If my brother or sister is dysfunctional, then so am I. The law of Christ commands that we do something for any member of the body that is in trouble. We cannot look away. We cannot act as if they don't exist. If you are there and God has allowed you to know about their struggle, He expects you to do one of two things. First, if you have the ability to pull them out of the struggle, then you must do so. Second, if you don't, then you must intercede for their deliverance. In God's eyes, their problem is all our problem.

Just like the natural body, the body of Christ has many members with different assignments. The scriptures give details about the members of the body and their assignments.

> Here are some of the parts God has appointed for the church: first are apostles, second are prophets, third are teachers, then those who do miracles, those who have the gift of healing, those who can help others, those who have the gift of leadership, those who speak in unknown languages. Are we all apostles? Are we all prophets? Are we all teachers? Do we all have the power to do miracles? Do we all have the gift of healing? Do we all have the ability to speak in unknown languages? Do we all have the ability to interpret unknown languages? Of course not! So you should earnestly desire the most helpful gifts. But now let me show you a way of life that is best of all. (1 Corinthians 12:28–31 NLT)

From this scripture, you see that there are many areas from which a member of the body can operate. It acknowledges that there are a variety of assignments, so we can't expect to all be given the same assignment. As you continue to 1 Corinthians 13, you will find out the way of life that is better. You will read that regardless of the assignment, the motive for operating has to be out of love. The foundation must be love of God and love of others. An assignment is never given so that the vessel can be seen or lifted up in pride. The assignment is given to push forward the plan of God, which always embodies love.

> Now these are the gifts Christ gave to the church: the apostles, the prophets, the evangelists, and the pastors and teachers. Their responsibility is to equip God's people to do his work and build up the church, the body of Christ. This will continue until we all come to such unity in our faith and knowledge of God's son that we will be mature in the Lord, measuring up to the full and complete standard of Christ. Then we will no longer be immature like children. We won't be tossed and blown about by every wind of new teaching. We will not be influenced when people try to trick us with lies so clever, they sound like the truth. Instead, we will speak the truth in love, growing in every way more and more like Christ, who is the head of his body, the church. He makes the whole body fit together perfectly. As each part, does its own special work. It helps the other parts grow, so that the whole body is healthy and growing and full of love. (Ephesians 4:11–16 NLT)

This scripture deals with the gifts that Christ gave to the church. Some call these gifts the fivefold ministers. Unfortunately, some churches have eliminated the apostle and the prophet as no longer needed and have thereby limited the growth of the members of the body connected with their church. All five of these gifts operate together to equip or train the people to do God's work that has been assigned to them for the building up of the body. When we eliminate any one of these gifts, it changes the dynamics and stunts the growth of the body. These gifts are to operate together until the body comes to unity—a unity where there is no separation because of denomination, theological disagreements, or ethnic background.

These five gifts are on assignment until the body is mature, looks like Christ, and is whole, healthy, and full of love. These gifts help the body to seek out their God-given assignment, their special work. They help each person see that God has given them something that they must do and encourages them to step out in faith to complete their assignment. They help each person see the spiritual requirement of obedience to the Word of God and the instruction given relating to their assignment. The scripture makes it clear that as each person does their assignment, it helps others in the body grow. We grow together or our growth is limited by our disobedience to God's set plan of growth.

> God has given each of you a gift from his great variety of spiritual gifts. Use them well to serve one another. Do you have the gift of speaking? Then speak as though God himself were speaking through you. Do you have the gift of helping others? Do it with all the strength and energy that God supplies. Then everything you do will bring glory to God through Jesus Christ. All glory and power to him forever and ever! Amen. (1 Peter 4:10–11 NLT)

Scripture confirms that each person has been given a gift to serve the body of Christ. And in our serving, we glorify God. Each person is needed. No one is just an extra, unusable part that is not needed. We all have a function. And how we function is to bring glory to God. God is waiting for us to go back to when there were no denominations and no personal agendas. When all people cared about was spreading the gospel and telling everyone that the kingdom of God is at hand. It was not about making your own name great and building your ministry. It was all about God. Until we all see what God is saying to us in the scripture about working together as one, we will never get to our ultimate anointing or efficiency.

CHAPTER 4

Functioning According to God's Plan

God gives us clear instructions on how He wants us to live with our brothers and sister in the body as well as with those outside the body. Ultimately, we are to personally grow while encouraging others in the body to grow, and at the same time taking every available opportunity to bring others outside the body into the body of Christ. Romans 12 provides a guide for doing all three:

1. Personal growth
2. Building the body of Christ
3. Adding to the body of Christ

And so, dear brothers and sister, I plead with you to give your bodies to God because of all he has done for you, let them be a living and holy sacrifice—the kind he will find acceptable. This is truly the way to worship him. Don't copy the behavior and customs of this world, but let God transform you into a new person by changing the way you think. Then you will learn to know God's will for you which is good and pleasing and perfect. Because of the privilege and authority God has given me, I give each of you this warning: Don't think you are better than you really are. Be honest in your evaluation of yourselves, measuring yourselves by the faith God has given us. Just as our bodies have many parts and each part has a special function, so it is with Christ's body. We are many parts of one body, and we all belong to each other. In his grace, God has given us different gifts for doing certain things well. So if God has given you the ability to prophesy, speak out with as much faith as God has given you. If your gift is serving others, serve them well. If you are a teacher, teach well. If your gift is to encourage others, be encouraging. If it is giving, give generously. If God has given you leadership ability, take the responsibility seriously. And if you have a gift for showing kindness to others, do it gladly. Don't just pretend to love others. Really love them. Hate what is wrong. Hold tightly to what is good. Love each other with genuine affection and take delight in honoring each other. Never be lazy but work hard and serve the Lord enthusiastically. Rejoice in our confident hope. Be patient in trouble and keep on praying. When God's people are in need be ready to help them. Always be eager to practice hospitality. Bless those who persecute you. Don't curse them, pray that God will bless them. Be happy with those who are happy and weep with those who weep. Live in harmony with each other. Don't be too proud to enjoy the company of ordinary people. And don't think you know it all. Never pay back evil with more evil. Do things in such a way that everyone can see you are honorable. Do all that you can to live in peace with everyone. Dear friends, never take revenge. Leave that to the righteous anger of God. For the scriptures say, "I will take revenge; I will pay them back" says the Lord. Instead, if your enemies are hungry, feed them. If they are thirsty, give them something to drink. In doing this, you will heap burning coals of shame on their heads. Don't let evil conquer you but conquer evil by doing good. (Romans 12 NLT)

This scripture tells us a lot about how God wants us to behave in many situations such as loving and providing for the needs of your enemy and praying for them instead of trying to get revenge. I believe this principle is important because, unfortunately, when asked about the enemies in our lives, many of our enemies are part of the body of Christ that have hurt us in the past. It is not wise to seek revenge and harm any part of the body because God commands us not to take revenge, but also in the long run, you will be affected as well. In addition, if your behavior toward someone outside the body shows a godly love, your response to them can be a drawing card that will cause them to choose a relationship with Jesus Christ.

As stated earlier, the scripture does provide guidance that will promote personal growth, build the body of Christ, and add to the body of Christ.

Personal growth

When we present ourselves to God to be a living sacrifice, the closeness to God that has to happen in order for one to be a living sacrifice will promote an increase in our spiritual and personal growth. Furthermore, the concept of allowing God to transform our thinking will give us the mind of Christ so that we will know God's will for our lives. And as a sacrifice, knowing God's will for our lives will enable us to walk that will out since our life is not governed by what we want but is governed by God's will. Personal growth is improving one's habits and behavior, actions, and reactions. If God is the governing factor of our habits, behavior, actions, and reactions, there can be nothing else but growth.

Building the body of Christ

Good relationships within the body of Christ that are peaceful and not competitive and not intertwined with jealousy make room for everyone to thrive. Everyone in these types of relationships feels free to be authentic and free to excel in whatever they are called to do. When each person can celebrate and encourage their brother and sister without feeling intimidated by their success, each person is helping to build up the body of Christ, and we will all benefit. We must embrace the reality that we all succeed when one succeeds.

Adding to the body of Christ

What draws those outside the body of Christ is not our message; it is the love that we display. The love and support we give to our brothers and sisters as well as the love we show to others. When onlookers can see you love your enemies and watch you bless those who persecute you, that is even a greater drawing card than just the love and hospitality they observe between brethren. Most people will, if given evil, will return evil. Yet most people would love to live in peace, though they will express that they don't feel that such peace is possible. But when a child of God can live in peace regardless of the situations around them, observers will definitely want to know where they can get some of what you have that allows your spirit to be so peaceful. It is the greatest example of what God can do in the life of someone who has allowed God to transform every element of their person.

I also appreciate that this scripture in Romans 12 speaks to the various assignments that God gives that do not include the fivefold ministers. There has been a great push over the years for many of the body of Christ to be accepted and proclaimed into one of the designated positions within the fivefold (apostle, prophet, evangelist, pastor, teacher). Trying to walk into one of these positions can be harmful if God has not placed you there. But this scripture clearly shows that there are many other areas that are just as, if not more important, to God. This scripture confirms the following gifts that God gives for people to do well:

- The gift of giving
- The gift of kindness
- The gift of encouraging
- The gift of help
- The gift of prophecy
- The gift of hospitality
- The gift of teaching
- The gift of leadership
- The gift of loving
- The gift of patience
- The gift of serving
- The gift of empathy

All of us have at some time experienced the ministry of someone who was giving, kind, encouraging, patient, loving, and could make you feel so loved and special as they just served you. Upon experiencing their ministry, we can all attest that our lives were positively affected by the loving care of those who were just doing what God had gifted them to do.

The body has to realize that there is no little assignment that is given out by God. Any and everything that God gifts you to do is needed and is important to Him. We can never look at our assignment or gifting as more important than another person's assignment or gifting. We can never look at our assignment or gifting as less than another person's assignment or gifting. Every part of the body is needed. As the scripture says, we are many parts of one body, and we all belong to each other. I need you, and you need me. The connection that God has created by making us one body is stronger than if we were physically next to each other. This connection transcends whether I know you or have even met you. I need to pray for you and uplift you in prayer even if I will never get to meet you on this side of heaven.

CHAPTER 5

Addressing Mindsets That Hinder Wholeness

Over the years of dealing with recovery, I have found that the initial step in the process of recovery is to look at and acknowledge that there is an issue from which one must recover. Acceptance of the problem is the beginning of correcting the problem. You can't fix what you won't acknowledge.

I question whether we can promote the oneness of the body of Christ without addressing the issue of prejudice within the body of Christ. How many times have we heard people attest that Sunday is the most segregated day of the week? I have heard it so much that I personally began to evaluate the validity of that comment. I have observed that the majority of churches consist of God's people coming together to worship God (the same God) with individuals that look like themselves. Not all churches are like this, and I salute those that are representative of all the ethnic groups in their community. Unfortunately, for the majority, our worship services are segregated.

Why are our churches segregated? I believe it is important to evaluate whether the segregation is a product of our community, a product of those we approach to share the good news of the gospel, or a product of some deep-seated prejudice. We should question why we are more comfortable with our own kind, and what factors determine how we evaluate *our own kind*. What characteristics, features, or behaviors are we looking at to gauge whether a person is *your own kind*? Isn't all mankind *our own kind*? Are there differences in mankind that place certain ones at a higher level, deserving of more than others? And if there are such differences, what are they? Could the differences that we see be an indication that there is a seed of prejudice in our heart that has been hidden; that we have neglected to see its fruit in operation?

Beginning in the sixth chapter of Genesis, God began to speak to Noah. God had found Noah to be the only righteous man remaining on earth. He charged Noah to prepare an ark, gather every animal and bird, and put his family and all the animals he had gathered into that ark. Because of the evil of all mankind, God was planning to destroy all mankind, and only Noah and his family would be left. After God destroyed all mankind in the flood, the world was replenished by the sons of Noah and their wives.

Noah had three sons, Japheth, Shem, and Ham. From these three came the various races of the world. Japheth was the father of the European and Euro-Asian; Shem was the father of the Semitic/Jewish races; and Ham was the father of the Afro-Asian races. Although all three were very different, they were yet brothers having the same father. Just as the body of Christ is different, made up of different races, we still all have one Father.

Our challenge today is to look past the outer appearances and realize that whatever the skin tone, whatever the race, we have the same Father, if we are a member of the body of Christ. We are related, and we have to care for, pray for, and intercede for every member of the body. The body of Christ trumps all other groups for which you are a member. It is the most important group to aspire to join.

One of the greatest things currently in this time is the mixture of races in families. The benefits of being associated with members of your family that represent a different race are what God wants for His children. And to be a product of more than one race is a blessing. A blessing of having the ability to relate to more than one racial group. I know that there is sometimes a struggle for people of mixed race, not being able to determine what group they most associate with. However, if embraced as a blessing, it helps one to recognize that we are more alike than we are different. As a member of the body of Christ that reads the same Bible, that structures our lives around the same principles of that Bible, and that serves the same God, we are connected. We are connected to God but also connected to each other.

The scripture speaks about the treatment of others involving partiality. Partiality is defined as unfair bias in favor of one thing or person compared with another. Similar words having the same meaning are *bias*, *prejudice*, and *favoritism*. Another phrase within the Bible used to speak about partiality is "respect of person."

> My dear brother and sister, how can you claim to have faith in our glorious Lord Jesus Christ if you favor some people over others? For example, suppose someone comes into your meeting dressed in fancy clothes and expensive jewelry, and another comes in who is poor and dressed in dirty clothes. If you give special attention and a good seat to the rich person, but you say to the poor one, "You can stand over there, or else sit on the floor"—well, doesn't this discrimination show that your judgments are guided by evil motions? Listen to me, dear brothers and sister. Hasn't God chosen the poor in this world to be rich in faith? Aren't they the ones who will inherit the Kingdom he promised to those who love him? But you dishonor the poor! Isn't it the rich who oppress you and drag you into court? Aren't they the ones who slander Jesus Christ, whose noble name you bear? Yes, indeed, it is good when you obey the royal law as found in the scripture. "Love your neighbor as yourself". But if you favor some people over others, you are committing a sin. You are guilty of breaking the law. (James 2:1–9 NLT)

Clearly, partiality and respecter of person are softer words and phrases, but the actions associated are still prejudice and racism, and

God speaks against that treatment toward others. As the body of Christ attempts to represent the love of God on earth and eliminate racism in our country, we must address how much racism/partiality is promoted by our own actions. Can we really say that we love and value all people the way God values them? If not, then why not? One of the things I stress as a counselor is the need to be introspective. We should always ask ourselves *why* when we look at how we feel, how we behave, and how we entreat others. We must ask the questions, "What is it in me that makes me uncomfortable around other races?" "What is it in me that allows me to make judgment calls on a person when I have not talked to them or taken the time to know them?"

The truth is that the world will not be able to overcome the evils of racism until the body of Christ overcomes its prejudices. We are the salt and the light of the world. If we don't purge ourselves of mindsets that are not aligned with God's mindset, how can we make a difference? Wholeness dictates that we love one another. God tells us in various places in His word to do just that: love one another, esteem others higher than ourselves. In other words, don't look down on or devalue another person. Let us, the body of Christ, be the first partakers of eliminating the mindset that results in prejudice and racism.

CHAPTER 6

Helping the Body Heal

Those in the body of Christ need an awakening and a mindset transition to understand and acknowledge how much we are all connected. Because we have spent so much time being separated and acting as separate entities, there is a healing that needs to take place.

Our healing journey cannot begin unless we are willing to challenge our old views and attitudes. And in case anyone reading this is about to start blaming others for any lack of success, be warned that this approach will not be accepted by God. Each of us is challenged to be our best self as we continue to support and encourage our brother and sister to be their best self. God has given us healing elements; I call *one another* commands to direct us on how we are to help each other through our healing process.

Element of love

The first and most mentioned *one another* in the Bible is to "love one another." The foundation of anything we do has to be built upon love. If love is not the foundation, then some selfish agenda will be the foundation for what we do.

> A new commandment I give to you, that you
> *love one another* as I have loved you, that you also
> *love one another*. By this all will know that you

are My disciples if you *have love for one another.* (John13:34–35 NKJV)

This is my commandment that you *love one another* as I have loved you. Greater love has no one than this than to lay down one's life for his friends. You are My friends if you do whatever I command you. No longer do I call you servants, for a servant does not know what his master is doing; but I have called you friends, for all things that I heard from My father I have made known to you. You did not choose Me, but I chose you and appointed you that you should go and bear fruit and that your fruit should remain, that whatever you ask the Father in My name He may give you. These things I command you that you *love one another.* (John 15:12–17 NKJV)

Both scriptures were the words of Jesus. Those who are his followers, his church, his body, must love. As God the Father gave the ten commandments, Jesus came and said that all the ten commandments are embodied in two commandments which are (1) to love God with all your heart and (2) to love our neighbor as we love ourselves. Jesus established that our connection to Him is directly affected by the love that we have for others. If we can't love others, we cannot love God. The two are interrelated. To love God in the way that He wants, we also must have in our heart the love for others. Others include all people, the lovable ones, the difficult ones, the ones that hate us, and the ones that we can't quite understand because of our various differences. The *one another* is all-inclusive of every human being.

"Jesus said to him, 'You shall love the Lord your God with all your heart, with your soul, and with all your mind. This is the first and great commandment. And the second is like it; You shall *love your neighbor* as yourself. On these two commandments hang all the Law and the Prophets'" (Matthew 22:37–40 NKJV).

Like the Pharisee that asked Jesus the question that caused him to respond giving the two greatest commandments, we must not get caught up on who is our neighbor. In God's mind, it is not the physical locale or connection, but it is the spiritual one of being part of the body. Our neighbor does not have to live in our city or even in our state or country. We may never have the opportunity to meet or know our neighbor by name. However, we are still to love. Hate cannot be an emotion that we experience toward another person under any situation.

In regard to loving one another, Paul tells us in Romans 13:8, "Owe no one anything except to *love one another* for he who loves another has fulfilled the law."

Peter speaks to loving one another "since you have purified your souls in obeying the truth through the Spirit in sincere love of the brethren, *love one another* fervently with a pure heart" (1 Peter 1:22).

John, the apostle who was one of the ones in Jesus's inner circle, not only spoke about loving one another in his writings in the Gospel but also in various other writings; he felt it prudent to speak about the necessity of loving one another.

> For this is the message that you heard from the beginning that we should *love one another*. (1 John 3:11 NKJV)

> And this is His commandment that we should believe on the name of His son Jesus Christ and *love one another*, as He gave us commandment. (1 John 3:23 NLT)

> Beloved let us *love one another* for love is of God; and everyone who loves is of God, and everyone who loves is born of God and knows God. He who does not love does not know God. (1 John 4:7–8 NKJV)

> Beloved if God so loved us, we also ought to *love one another*. No one has seen God at any time. If

we *love one another*, God abides in us and His love has been perfected in us. (1 John 4:11–12 NKJV)

The process of healing the body so that we can become one cannot begin until love is perfected in each member of the body.

Element of forgiving

Offenses are the major cause of separation in the body. Offenses are a breach of a law and illegal act, an annoyance or resentment brought about by a perceived insult to and disregard for oneself or one's standards or principles. For the body to come together, we must forgive one another. Forgiving is so important that God says if we will not forgive others, He won't forgive us our sins. There is nothing that is so offensive that we cannot forgive. Forgiveness is not optional. We are to forgive the person and let God handle the offense. In the Bible, the word used for offenses is *trespass*. Trespass means to enter the owner's land or property without permission; to commit an offense against a person or a set of rules.

> For if ye forgive men their trespasses, your heavenly Father will also forgive you. But if ye forgive not men their trespasses, neither will your Father forgive your trespasses. (Matthew 6:14–15)

> And when ye stand praying, forgive, if you have ought against any; that your Father also which is in heaven may forgive you your trespasses. But if ye do not forgive, neither will your Father which is in heaven forgive your trespasses. (Mark 11:25–26)

These scriptures clearly show that to the extent we are willing to forgive, that is the same measure that forgiveness will be extended to us by God. God expects us to be forgiving toward those who hurt us, especially a brother or sister.

> And be ye kind one to another, tenderhearted, *forgiving one another*, even as God for Christ's sake hath forgiven you. (Ephesians 4:32)

> Forbearing one another, and *forgiving one another*, if any have a quarrel against any: even as Christ forgave you, so also do ye. (Colossians 3:13)

Unless we master the first two elements of love and forgiveness, it will be hard to continue through to all the other elements that will heal the body. It is what we must strive to do if we are to heal and move forward together as one.

Element of kindness

Closely related to love is kindness. Kindness is the quality of being friendly, generous, and considerate. When there is no love, there is no kindness. Being kind is the result of having love for someone. A tender heart toward others is what allows us to be kind and considerate of others.

> Be *kindly affectionate to one another* with brotherly love, in honor giving preference to one another. (Romans 12:10)

> And be *kind to one another*, tender-hearted, forgiving one another, even as God in Christ forgave you. (Ephesians 4:32)

Element of like-mindedness

Because each member of the body has a different assignment, the way each one thinks and the things that concern them may be different. However, God wants us to be like-minded regarding the things of God and His kingdom agenda. He especially wants us to be in agreement about what the Word of God says. It has been our different thoughts and opinions that have resulted in the various denominations. These denominations were established because of disagreement about the Word and have further separated the body of Christ. Philippians 2:5 tells us, "Let this mind be in you, which was also in Christ Jesus."

If you run into conflict, the body of Christ, together, must seek the mind of God in any situation. We see in the Book of Acts, chapter 15, where the leaders did just that. They came together to discuss and reach an agreement on whether Gentiles, that were now being filled with the Holy Spirit, had to succumb to the rules under the law that all Jews had to abide by, specifically circumcision. They came together, discussed the pros and cons, prayed, and then reached an agreed-upon conclusion. God never intended us to come up with our own conclusion without consulting the Holy Spirit in prayer and waiting for an answer.

> Be of the *same mind toward one another*. Do not set your mind on high things, but associate with the humble. Do not be wise in your own opinion. (Romans 12:16 NKJV)

> Now may the God of patience and comfort grant you to *be like-minded toward one another* according to Christ Jesus that you may with one mind and one mouth glorify the God and Father of our Lord Jesus Christ. (Romans 15:5–6 NKJV)

Element of not judging

Many of the body of Christ do not associate with other members of the body because they have judged them. In their opinion, that member or group of members have ideas and/or behaviors that have been deemed unacceptable. Being judgmental is having an excessively critical point of view. It stops us from praying for that person or persons, and it also does not make provision for personal growth and change. All of us at some point in our life have said or done something that we are not proud of, would be embarrassed if others knew, and are grateful that a final conclusion of who we are was not determined by the things we did in our past. We must allow for God to come into a person's life to change them as he has changed us. We should never be responsible for shutting the door on another person's potential to excel to another level. When we judge, we make a final decision regarding another member of the body that places them in a position, in our minds, that says that they can never change.

Our opinion then cuts them off from ever moving forward and being used by God, especially if we take it upon ourselves to share our opinion about that person with others who have the ability to stop them from moving forward in the kingdom of God. In the natural, it is synonymous to a doctor giving you a report that your leg or arm or hand will never be usable again. It could stop you from using that particular part of the body and make it weaker as well as affect other portions of your body that have to compensate for that weaker or unusable member. Not accepting the report and making that member accountable for change and pushing that member to do what it is they are supposed to do can be the catalyst for positive change, both naturally and spiritually.

> *Judge not*, and you shall not be judged. Condemn not and you shall not be condemned. Forgive and you will be forgiven. (Luke 6:37 NKJV)

> Therefore, let us *not judge one another* anymore, but rather resolve this not to put a stumbling block or a cause to fall in our brother's way. (Romans 14:13 NKJV)

> There is one lawgiver, who is able to save and to destroy, who art thou that *judgest another?* (James 4:12)

Element of edifying and exhorting

This element helps the member of the body grow. To exhort means to strongly encourage or urge someone to do something. Each member should exhort other members to be their best and to do their best in the assignment God has given them. To edify is to instruct or improve orally or intellectually. We are to be helpers one to another and not watch another member struggle in an area when we have the ability to assist them in becoming their best self.

> Therefore, let us pursue the things which make for peace and the things by which one may *edify another*. (Romans 14:19 NKJV)

> Beware, brethren, lest there be in any of you an evil heart of unbelief in departing from the living God; but *exhort one another* daily, while it is called "Today" lest any of you be hardened through the deceitfulness of sin. (Hebrews 3:12–13 NKJV)

> And let us consider one another in order to stir up love and good works, not forsaking the assembling of ourselves together, as in the manner of some but *exhorting one another* and so much the more as you see the Day approaching. (Hebrews 10:24–25 NKJV)

Element of acceptance

Every person has a desire to be accepted and received by others as a viable part of a group. Our souls are adversely affected by rejection at any age and by any person. We all want to be received. How much more important than to be received into the body of Christ as a member that is needed, appreciated, and valued. Not because of who we are or what we have but because of the love that God has for us.

"Therefore *receive one another* just as Christ also received us to the glory of God" (Romans 15:7 NKJV).

Element of admonishment

Admonish means to warn and reprimand. It is quite different from judgment because it uses the Word of God to show someone the error of their ways. It is not done in judgment, but it is done in love with the idea of helping a brother and sister get closer to God and their destiny. It is important that admonishment comes from one who is walking according to the Word; otherwise, it becomes not a correction but judgment.

> Now I myself, am confident concerning you my brethren, that you also are full of goodness, filled with all knowledge, able also to *admonish one another*. (Romans 15:14 NKJV)

> Let the Word of Christ dwell in you richly in all wisdom, teaching, and *admonishing one another* in psalms and hymns and spiritual songs, singing with grace in your hearts to the Lord. (Colossians 3:16 NKJV)

Element of caring

Caring for one another in the body of Christ knits us closer together into the oneness that God desires. Caring embodies forbearing, which is being patient and having restraint so as not to come against another member of the body in a harsh way. Caring also includes empathy and understanding for the why and root of behavior displayed by a member that may be offensive to you. Caring is concern about the condition of another member in the body and not walking away, justifying your behavior as *the issue is their problem* alone and none of your business.

That there should be no schism in the body, but that the member should have the same *care for one another*. (1 Corinthians 12:25 NKJV)

With all lowliness and gentleness, with longsuffering, *bearing with one another in love*, endeavoring to keep the unity of the Spirit in the bond of peace. (Ephesians 4:2–3 NKJV)

Therefore, as the elect of God, holy and beloved, put on tender mercies, kindness, humility, meekness, longsuffering, *bearing with one another* and forgiving one another. If anyone has a complaint against another; even as Christ forgave you, so you also must do. (Colossians 3:12–13 NKJV)

Element of serving and restoring

Jesus's three years of ministry was about serving those in need and restoring those not connected with God to a more connected relationship with God. As the body of Christ learns to imitate Jesus and love others like we have been commanded to do, the natural effect will move us into serving and restoring others. Seeing a need and responding to it and providing resources at our disposal to meet a need will all become a natural reaction. If we chose, however, to watch our brother or sister struggle and even contribute to their burden by talking about them, we will suffer a loss as they suffer a loss. We are not unaffected by the struggles of another member of the body. Where they are weak, we are also weak. And where they are strong, we are by the same, strong in that area as well.

For you, brethren, have been called to liberty; only do not use liberty as an opportunity for the flesh but through love *serve one another*. For all the law is fulfilled in one word, even in this; "You shall love your neighbor as yourself". But if you bite and devour one another beware lest you be consumed by one another. (Galatians 5:13–15 NKJV)

Brethren, if a man is overtaken in any trespass, you who are spiritual *restore such a one* in a spirit of gentleness, considering yourself lest you also be tempted. Bear one another's burden and so fulfill the law of Christ. (Galatians 6:1–2 NKJV*)*

As we come to know about a brother or sister's personal struggle, we must first evaluate whether we are spiritual and thus have the compassion of Christ to restore them. We must approach them with gentleness and not judgment, considering how we would want to be treated in the midst of our own struggle. Part of restoring involves bearing our brother's burdens. Bearing their burdens means walking alongside your brother and helping them to shoulder the weight of it. Doing this fulfills the law of Christ.

What is the law of Christ mentioned in this scripture? It is first mentioned by Jesus in Matthew 22:36–40. And that law continues to be referred to throughout the New Testament.

Then one of them, a lawyer, asked Him a question, testing Him, and saying, "Teacher, which is the great commandment in the law"? Jesus said to him, "You shall love the Lord your God with all your heart, with all your soul and with all your mind. This is the first and great commandment. And the second is like it: You shall love your neighbor as yourself, on these two commandments hang all the Law and the Prophets". (Matthew 22:35–40)

The law of Christ appears simple, just two commandments. Love God will all that is within you and love your neighbor as you love yourself. Simplicity is not in the number of commandments because these two commandments govern every thought, action, behavior, attitude, or statement that can be made by a person. Love of God or love of others must be the foundation of all that is done. However, how many times do we make decisions from our own self-interest? How often do we do what is best for ourselves and not considering others that may be adversely affected by our decision? Deciding from this vantage point is in direct conflict with the law of Christ. To walk according to these two commandments takes a renewing of the mind.

> Finally, all of you be of one mind having compassion for one another; love as brothers, be tenderhearted, be courteous, not returning evil for evil or reviling for reviling, but on the contrary blessing, knowing that you were called to this, that you may inherit a blessing. (1 Peter 3:8–9 NKJV)

> As each one has received a gift, minister it to one another as good stewards of the manifold grace of God. (1 Peter 4:10 NKJV)

> Confess your trespasses to one another and pray for one another that you may be healed. The effective, fervent prayer of a righteous man avails much. Elijah was a man with a nature like ours, and he prayed earnestly that it would not rain, and the earth produced its fruit. Brethren, if anyone among you wanders from the truth, and someone turns him back, let him know that he turns a sinner from the error of his way, will save a soul from death and cover a multitude of sins. (James 5:16–20 NKJV)

This element requires that members of the body have a selfless and compassionate walk as they continue to operate in their assigned places.

Element of submission

The element of submitting one to another takes away the destructive element of control. We cannot administer our control over other members of the body and submit to them at the same time. There are positions in the body of Christ that do control other parts as they both operate according to their calling. As the brain controls other parts of the natural body, it does so because of what it was created to do, not because it wishes to excel above the other members of the body. Those that are called to headship position (apostle, prophet, evangelist, pastor, teacher) must also operate in the same manner. They are called for the perfecting of the body, not for abusing the body. They control because that is what they are called to do, not because they are trying to excel over others. They must do what they are called to do yet consider and operate according to the law of Christ, a law that requires love and selflessness.

> *Submitting to one another* in the fear of God.
> (Ephesians 5:21 NKJV)

> Likewise, you younger people *submit yourselves* to your elders. Yes, all of you be *submissive to one another*, and be clothed with humility for God resists the proud but gives grace to the humble.
> (1 Peter 5:5 NKJV)

Element of comfort

Comfort is the easing or alleviation of a person's feelings of grief or distress. We are expected to provide comfort to those that need it. It is an act of service as well as the character of the Holy Spirit. Jesus on various occasions spoke about the coming of a comforter that was to come. As the Holy Spirit leads, He will use us, the body of Christ, to comfort those in need.

Therefore *comfort each other* and edify one another, just as you also are doing. (1 Thessalonians 5:11 NKJV)

And above all things have fervent love for one another, for love will cover a multitude of sins. Be hospitable to one another without grumbling. (1 Peter 4:8–9 NKJV)

All these elements are needed and should be operating in the body of Christ as we journey down the path of healing, to the place of oneness. Until we are really one body united in Christ, we are still in need of healing.

CHAPTER 7

Unity the Ultimate Goal

And he gave some, apostles; and some, prophets; and some,
evangelists; and some pastors and teachers; For the perfecting
of the saints, for the work of the ministry, for the edifying
of the body of Christ: Till we all come in the unity of faith,
and of the knowledge of the Son of God, unto a perfect man,
unto the measure of the stature of the fullness of Christ.
—Ephesians 4:11–13

As the body of Christ works toward becoming whole, the level of unity rises. In Ephesians 4:11–13, it says that God set certain ministers in place with the purpose of them equipping the saints until we all come to the unity of the faith and of the knowledge of the Son of God.

Healing must take place first. When all elements are operating in each member, we will be mature. What does maturity look like? It has nothing to do with the number of years a person has been living or the number of years a person has been in church. Maturity is when we have learned to operate as one but in our different capacities. Whereby we move, think, and act as one body.

We can get a better understanding of this as we look at what happens as a baby matures enough to first sit up and then stand and finally, balance themselves before taking steps. As I watched my youngest grandchild go through this process, I noticed the many parts of her body that assisted in this process. For a baby to sit up, the muscles that need to be operating are not just the muscles in the baby's back. The neck muscles have to be operating to keep the head sturdy so that the baby will not wobble back and forth. The stomach muscles must also be strong enough to stop the baby from falling backward. As the baby stands, more muscle in the back and legs must be operational, as well as muscles in the ankles and feet. In addition, the brain must be developed enough to help the body stay balanced. Then as the baby walks, all these muscles plus the upper body must work in unity with one purpose and one goal so that the baby will walk, run, and later have the ability to skip.

We will know when the body of Christ is mature when we all operate in unity; when every church in a city is united to impact that city; when every church in a state works together to have a state-wide impact. As we see this type of cooperation, we will know that the body of Christ has reached maturity. When the agenda of God takes precedence over each leader's personal agenda, then the body of Christ has reached maturity and has acquired unity.

What do we lose if we continue in the same manner? You may say this has been working for years; why change things now? Why try to fix something that you do not think is broken? You may feel that everyone looking toward their own interest and not considering others is the way things are done and the way they have always been done. But does that make it acceptable to God? Is there a real cost of remaining the same and not trying to move toward wholeness for the body of Christ?

> Behold how good and how pleasant it is for brethren to dwell together in unity. It is like the precious ointment upon the head, that ran down upon the beard, even Aaron's beard; that went down to the skirts of his garments; as the dew of Hermon, and as the dew that descended upon the mountains of Zion for there the Lord commanded the blessings, even life for evermore. (Psalm 133 NKJV)

This scripture tells us that unity is good and pleasant. Unity is compared to two things: (1) the ointment that ran down Aaron's beard and (2) the dew of Hermon that descends upon the mountain of Zion. But most importantly, it reminds us that when there is unity, God commands blessings and life in the midst of unity.

The precious ointment that ran down from Aaron's head to his beard and down to his skirt is the first comparison. What is the significance of this comparison? Aaron represents the priesthood. The leadership anointed by God to minister to Him. The Aaronic Priesthood were the priests who served the altar and exclusively handled the holy things. They were in charge of offerings and sacrifices. They were the ones that entered the holy of holies. Being instated into this ministry involved the pouring of oil on the top of the head of the person installed. That oil represented God's call and confirmation to operate as a priest to Him. The natural progression of anything poured is to run down. The oil poured on Aaron's head progressed down his face, onto his beard, and finally down his clothes to the hem of his garment (which garment was specific to the ministry).

Unity is alignment. Alignment is defined as (1) arrangement in a straight line, or in correct or appropriate relative positions and (2) a position of agreement or alliance. When things are aligned, what comes from the top will fall on those aligned with it. The anointing falls from the top down to all that are aligned. If we are not in alignment with our leaders that are appointed by God, we will miss what is flowing down from them because of our misalignment.

When we look at the history of the church, the lack of unity, and the various denominations, the cause was not being aligned with the leadership. Over the years, people who walked together in ministry reached areas of disagreement. When conflicts could not be resolved, alignment became nonexistent. As a result, supporting leaders moved on to establish other religious organizations that promoted their ideology. Currently, we have more than two hundred Christian denominations in the US and forty-five thousand globally according to the Center for the Study of Global Christianity (February 27, 2021—http://www.livescience.com).

In order for all these denominations to reach unity, we will have to focus on what we have in common and not concern ourselves with those ideas and interpretations of the scriptures that are not aligned. Our common ground is that we are the body of Christ, and we have one head, Jesus Christ. If we move ourselves out of the way and allow Him to direct us, alignment and unity can be achieved. And please allow me, by permission of the Holy Spirit, to say that it is not our assignment to judge whether our brother or sister is truly part of the body. We do not get to make that assessment. God will decide. We must accept their assertion that they have accepted Jesus Christ and not disregard them because they do not come up to our standard. If their behavior offends you, then God is allowing you to be affected to either pray for their deliverance or to walk alongside them in their journey of deliverance. You must assess yourself to evaluate if you are spiritual enough to do so by God's wisdom and direction.

"Brethren, if a man be overtaken in a fault, ye which are spiritual restore such a one in the spirit of meekness, considering thyself, lest thou also be tempted" (Galatians 6:1).

The second comparison involves both Mount Hermon and the mountains of Zion. Mount Hermon represents the favor of God and the resulting victories. It was through various battles recorded in Deuteronomy, Joshua, and 1 Chronicles that God gave the Israelites victories which allowed them to obtain pieces of the land around Mount Hermon with every battle won until all the land was theirs. The dew coming up from Mount Hermon is the blessings that come from the favor of God that then descends to the mountains of Zion.

Mount Zion is the place where Yahweh, the God of Israel, dwelled according to scriptures.

> Sing praises to the Lord, who dwells in Zion! Declare His deeds among the people. (Psalm 9:11 NKJV)

> In Judah God is known; His name is great in Israel. In Salem also is His tabernacle and His dwelling place in Zion. (Psalm 76:1–2 NKJV)

Zion is a specific historically important location. Spiritually it is important because it was where God's presence was on the earth. The name Zion refers to both a hill in the city of Jerusalem and to the city of Zion. Zion is used in a general way, spiritually, to mean *holy place* or *kingdom of heaven*. In various scriptures, the children of God are referred to as *the daughter of Zion* or *the sons of Zion*. Therefore, Zion not only represents the place where God dwells, but also the community of God's people with whom He dwells. If God is present in a place, then confusion and conflict cannot be in that place, so unity will prevail.

This second comparison to unity is the favor of God that provides blessings to the people of God that dwell in God's presence. The implication of dwelling together in the place where God dwells is oneness of thought and purpose, which creates unity.

God wants to declare blessings on His people, but our blessings are limited. They are limited because we are not united. The extent of the blessings is correlated to the unity and alignment to God and to each other. Yes, we experience blessings, but eyes have not seen, or ears heard of what God would like to do for us when we are mature and united as one body. We cannot conceive what we are losing in God as we continue to operate in the manner that we have always operated. Some may say that you can't miss what you do not know about, but I disagree. Because we are connected to God, there is a pulling and a knowing that there is more, even if we do not know what it looks like in the natural.

In 2 Chronicles 5, the king, all levels of ministry, all levels of leadership, and the congregation were all on one accord (united) to gather and put into the temple the ark, the tabernacle of meetings, and all the holy furnishing in place. When they were done, they all praised the Lord together. As they worship, the house of the Lord was filled with a cloud and the glory of the Lord filled the house of God. God's glory came as a result of the unity of the people. Everybody from the king down worked and then they all worshipped God together. It was not just the verbal worship that drew God's presence. It was also the worship of unity. When our actions meet God's requirements, his commands, that is also worship. From the leaders down to the congregation, all must work together with one cause and one purpose. That is what unity looks like.

God is calling us to a place of maturity where every person that is called the *body of Christ* moves in unity. A place of wholeness where we think and act the same. If we want to see the full blessings of God flow, we have to be in unity. Unity in such a way that we celebrate each other's successes. Unity whereby we participate in the fight of deliverance for every member of the body that is struggling in any area. Unity where we participate in deliverance in a manner where we are willing, if necessary, to carry our brother or sister to the feet of Jesus.

There is a great, end-time blessing coming as we unite as instructed by God. There is a great blessing coming when we strive to be keepers of the body.

ABOUT THE AUTHOR

Diane White was born and raised in Oakland, California. She has been married for thirty-eight years and is the mother of two sons and grandmother of twelve. She retired as a corporate auditor from the federal government. She earned a bachelor of science in accounting, a doctorate in Christian counseling, and recently received her board certification as a master mental health coach. Diane, along with her husband, founded Tree of Life Restoration Ministries where she serves as pastor, and Extending a Hand Community Outreach Missions Inc., a nonprofit where she serves as counselor for the counseling center, case manager for the homeless coalition, and instructor for the leadership development courses. She works part-time for Sister-to-Sister DBA Serenity House, a women's dual diagnosis drug recovery program. There she is the program director and is responsible for counseling and teaching group on anger management and recovery from domestic violence. She is also the founder of Sarah's Daughters, a nonprofit organization whose goal is to empower women in every area of their lives. Within this organization, Diane and several other intercessors have started the Remanent Warriors Uprising School of Prayer. The author published her first book, *The Great Replacement: Strategic End Time Intercessory Warfare,* in 2021.